EX MAC

POWER DOWN

CREDITS

BRIAN K. VAUGHAN:
WRITER

TONY HARRIS:
PENCILS

JIM CLARK:
INKS

JD METTLER:
COLORS

JARED K. FLETCHER:
LETTERS

LEGAL

Jim Lee, *Editorial Director*
John Nee, *VP—Business Development*
Ben Abernathy, *Editor*
Kristy Quinn, *Assistant Editor*
Ed Roeder, *Art Director*
Paul Levitz, *President & Publisher*
Georg Brewer, *VP—Design & DC Direct Creative*
Richard Bruning, *Senior VP—Creative Director*
Patrick Caldon, *Executive VP—Finance & Operations*
Chris Caramalis, *VP—Finance*
John Cunningham, *VP—Marketing*
Terri Cunningham, *VP—Managing Editor*
Stephanie Fierman, *Senior VP—Sales & Marketing*
Alison Gill, *VP—Manufacturing*
Hank Kanalz, *VP—General Manager, WildStorm*
Lillian Laserson, *Senior VP & General Counsel*
Paula Lowitt, *Senior VP—Business & Legal Affairs*
MaryEllen McLaughlin, *VP—Advertising & Custom Publishing*
Gregory Noveck, *Senior VP—Creative Affairs*
Cheryl Rubin, *Senior VP—Brand Management*
Jeff Trojan, *VP—Business Development, DC Direct*
Bob Wayne, *VP—Sales*

Chapter 1

Power Down part 1

TUESDAY, SEPTEMBER 11, 2001

MY LAST BOYFRIEND WAS A CANUCK, AND HE ALWAYS TOOK CREDIT FOR THAT.

TIME TO PUNCH OUT ALREADY, JAN?

YOU GOT IN AT FOUR A.M. THIS MORNING, SIR. DEPUTY MAYOR WYLIE SCREAMS AT ME IF I LET YOU STAY INSIDE CITY HALL MORE THAN TWELVE HOURS AT A TIME.

WHAT'S WITH THE UMBRELLA, JANUARY? FORECAST WAS FOR NOTHING BUT A *HEAT WAVE* THIS WHOLE WEEK.

YEAH, BUT I SAW A FEW FLASHES OF *LIGHTNING* ON MY WAY IN.

AND THE LOCAL WEATHERMEN HAVE SUCKED WAY WORSE THAN USUAL FOR THE LAST FOUR YEARS OR SO.

I BLAME GLOBAL WARMING.

JOURNAL MOORE. HER SISTER *JANUARY* HAS BEEN INTERNING FOR US, ACTUALLY. I JUST PROMOTED HER TO MY EXECUTIVE ASSISTANT LAST WEEK.

JANUARY?

HEY, DAD SADDLED US WITH AN *INTEGER*, SO I DON'T ASK QUESTIONS ABOUT OTHER PEOPLE'S CRAZY NAMES.

HOW'S READJUSTING TO LIFE IN THE BIG APPLE BEEN?

JUST BUSY WITH MY VOLUNTEER WORK. I'VE BEEN BUSTING MY HUMP TRYING TO GET YOU THE *OLYMPICS* IN 2012.

THANKS, BUT IT'S A *PIPE DREAM*, AND NOT JUST BECAUSE OF SECURITY CONCERNS.

VANCOUVER JUST WON THE BID FOR THE 2010 WINTER OLYMPICS, AND THE I.O.C. DOESN'T LIKE TO HOST CONSECUTIVE GAMES ON THE SAME CONTINENT. BESIDES, THE U.S. SPENT WHATEVER GOODWILL WE STORED UP AFTER 9/11 ON IRAQ AND...

...WHEN DID YOU GO TO THE FALLS WITH *KREMLIN?*

WHAT DID YOU DO TO THE *LIGHTS?*

NOTHING. YOU MUST HAVE BLOWN A FUSE OR SOMETHING.

NOPE, THE WHOLE *BLOCK* IS OUT.

HOLD ON, THIS ONE'S ON *BATTERIES.*

--WITH INITIAL REPORTS INDICATING THAT THE CITYWIDE BLACKOUT HAS PARALYZED THIRTY-FIVE LONG ISLAND RAILROADS AND THE ENTIRE SUBWAY SYSTEM.

MAKING MATTERS WORSE, THE NINETY-DEGREE HEAT--

GODDAMN IT ALL. VOLUME UP.

NUH-UH, RAY SAID PEOPLE ARE STEALING STUFF AND SETTING FIRE TO ALL THE BUILDINGS IN THE BRONX.

RAY IS A *SNOB*, MITCHELL. IT'S NOT JUST OUR NEIGHBORHOOD, THIS IS HAPPENING ALL *OVER* NEW YORK, OKAY?

WELL, THAT DOESN'T MAKE ME FEEL BETTER!

I'M SORRY, HONEY. I DON'T *KNOW* WHY EVERYONE IS ACTING CRAZY.

THE LIGHTS WENT OUT LIKE THIS IN '65, BUT THE CITY WAS NICE AND CALM. YOUR FATHER AND I JUST...WE JUST TOOK THE TIME TO ENJOY EACH OTHER'S COMPANY.

WHY DO YOU ALWAYS MAKE IT SOUND LIKE EVERYTHING WAS BETTER BEFORE *I* WAS BORN?

IT'S NOT ABOUT YOU, MITCHELL.

THERE WAS JUST MORE... *CIVILITY* BACK THEN. WE STILL HAD RESPECT FOR AUTHORITY, I GUESS.

THIS IS WHAT HAPPENS WHEN NO ONE TRUSTS THE PEOPLE IN POWER.

COMPUTER...?

COMPUTER, T.V., 'FRIGERATOR.

ELECTRICITY IS OUT ALL OVER. AND YOU WATCH, OUR NEIGHBORHOOD WILL GET FIXED LAST, JUST 'CAUSE YOU PEOPLE ARE RACIST AGAINST ALL THE COLOREDS THAT LIVE OUT HERE.

OF COURSE.

BHOTA, CAN YOU REACH A SON-SPOT?

THE REGIONAL EQUIVALENT, YES.

THE HECK DID THEY DO TO YOUR EYES?

I HAVE NO IDEA WHAT YOU'RE TALKING ABOUT.

BUT SOME OF THESE MANHOLE COVERS HAVE BEEN ELECTRIFIED, SO I NEED YOU TO STAY INSIDE, ALL RIGHT?

POOR BASTARD.

I HAVE TO GET TO CITY HALL.

UH...

WHAT? OH, RIGHT, I'M DRESSED LIKE A BLASTED *MARTIAN*. I CAN'T...SORRY, I CAN'T CONCENTRATE ON...WHAT WAS I SAYING?

CITY HALL?

NOT LIKE THIS. WHERE ARE WE, ANYWAY?

SOUTHERN TIER OF BROOKLYN. NOT FAR FROM WHERE OUR JOURNEY BEGAN.

THAT'S THE MOST WRONG YOU'VE EVER BEEN, BHOTA. BUT GOOD, BROOKLYN IS GOOD.

WE'LL START WITH THE RUSSIAN.

HSSSSSS

NAJEBANYE!

I SHOULD PUT YOU IN *STEW* FOR THAT, MISS OCTOBER. WHAT KIND OF STUPID FUCKING CAT IS AFRAID OF *DARK*, ANYWAY?

AND HOW DOES BRADBURY TALK ME INTO *BABY-SITTING* FOR YOU WHEN HE KNOWS I HATE--

KLICK

HELLO...?

I ALWAYS KNEW THIS PLACE WOULD BE THE DEATH OF ME.

JUST HANG TIGHT, DAVE. I'D USE MY "ABILITIES," BUT, UH...

...IT WOULDN'T BE FAIR TO OUR CONSTITUENTS IN THE SAME SITUATION. I UNDERSTAND COMPLETELY, SIR.

SCOOT AND I WILL BE FINE.

WHO THE HELL IS "SCOOT"?

THAT CLERICAL WORKER WHO PLAYS SOLITAIRE AT HIS DESK ALL DAY.

IT HAPPENED ONCE! AND I WAS ON MY LUNCH BREAK!

WELL, MAYBE YOU'VE MADE A LOVE CONNECTION.

YOU KNOW WHAT HAPPENED NINE MONTHS AFTER THE LAST BLACKOUT.

ACTUALLY, THE BIRTH RATE WENT DOWN THAT YEAR, SIR.

JUST TELLING YOU WHAT WE THINK WE KNOW, MR. MAYOR.

AND WHAT DO YOU *THINK* YOU KNOW ABOUT OUR NUCLEAR PLANTS?

THE TWO INDIAN POINT REACTORS, NINE MILE, GINNA, AND FITZPATRICK ARE ALL SHUT DOWN UNTIL EVERYONE ELSE GOES OFF SAFE MODE.

WALL STREET? UNITED NATIONS?

BOTH CLOSED FOR BUSINESS, SIR.

THEN WHY THE HOLY FUCK HASN'T THE GOVERNOR DECLARED A STATE OF EMERGENCY?

ABOVE MY PAY GRADE, MAYOR HUNDRED.

PRICK IS PROBABLY WAITING UNTIL THE NETWORKS GET THEIR *LOCAL FEEDS* BACK BEFORE HE REARS HIS BALDING--

DEET DA DEET

IGNORE CALL.

DEET DA DEET

IGNORE CALL, DAMMIT.

EX MACHINA

Chapter 3   **Power Down** *part 3*

SATURDAY, MARCH 11, 2000

OWW!

SON OF A BASTARD!

UHNF!

YOU KNOW OUR ORDERS.

NO MERCY.

TRIGGER LOCK!

UNLESS YOU KNOW HOW TO TURN OFF A *KNIFE* WITH YOUR VOICE.

DON'T GET COCKY, BRADBURY. NEXT TIME, I'LL REMEMBER TO KILL ANY FLASHLIGHTS IN THE ROOM *FIRST*.

THERE WILL NOT *BE* NEXT TIME IF YOU CONTINUE TO TREAT TRAINING EXERCISE AS *STAGE PLAY*, MITCHELL.

LESS TALK, MORE FIGHT. YOU DO NOT SOUND SCARY WHEN YOU SAY DUMB CRAP LIKE "HOPE YOU ARE NOT AFRAID OF DARK."

AND WHAT WAS THAT STUPID MOVE WITH WINDOW?

I THOUGHT I'D GO WITH THE ELEMENT OF SURPRISE THIS TIME, KREMLIN. I'M JUST TRYING TO FIND NEW WAYS TO USE MY ABILITIES, OKAY?

WELL, IT'S A GOOD THING YOU GOT THOSE SUPERPOWERS, MITCH.

'CAUSE YOU PUNCH LIKE A *FAGGOT*.

THURSDAY, AUGUST 14, 2003

SCREEEEECH

WATCH IT! WATCH--

HOLY CRAP, IT'S *DAWN OF THE DEAD* OUT HERE, YO.

SO YOU REALLY WANT TO DO THIS?

HELLS, YEAH. NYPD'S GOT BIGGER STUFF TO WORRY ABOUT.

LET'S GO SHOPPING.

I HOPE THIS WAS WORTH IT, BOSS!

I DON'T KNOW WHY YOU COULDN'T WAIT ANOTHER HOUR FOR A *COPTER* TO GET YOU PAST THE TRAFFIC, BUT I HAD TO CALL IN EVERY FAVOR I HAD LEFT WITH THE HARBOR PATROL TO SCORE US A *GO-FAST BOAT.*

"GO-FAST" IS A PRETTY GAY NAME FOR SUCH A SWEET RIDE, HUH?

I MEAN, IT'S NOT LIKE THEY CALL F-16s "FLY-HIGH" PLANES OR FERRARIS--

I LOST MY POWERS, BRADBURY.

YOU GOT *SHITCANNED?*

MY "SUPER" POWERS, NOT MY MAYORAL ONES. I STOPPED BEING ABLE TO COMMUNICATE WITH MACHINES RIGHT WHEN THE BLACKOUT HIT.

I DON'T KNOW HOW OR WHY, BUT I THINK THE MAN I'M GOING TO SEE MIGHT HAVE ANSWERS.

WHO IS THIS GUY? ARE WE GONNA KICK HIS ASS?

WE AREN'T GOING TO DO ANYTHING, BRADBURY.

I KNOW THIS GOES AGAINST EVERY FIBER OF YOUR BEING, BUT YOU HAVE TO LET ME DO THIS ONE SOLO.

FUCK THAT! I'M SICK OF GETTING SHUT OUT, *SIR!* EVERY TIME I AM, THINGS GO ROTTEN!

I HAVE A *JOB* TO DO! WHY DON'T YOU TRUST ME TO DO IT?

RICK, THERE'S A REASON YOU'RE THE ONLY PERSON ALIVE WHO KNOWS THE ONE THING ABOUT ME THAT *NOBODY* ELSE DOES, NOT KREMLIN, NOT MY MOTHER, NOT ANYONE.

I TRUST YOU COMPLETELY... BUT I NEED YOU TO TRUST ME, TOO.

HNNNN...

I'M VERY SORRY ABOUT YOUR COMPANION, MA'AM.

FOR WHAT LITTLE IT'S WORTH, I TRIED TO WARN HIM THAT MY *ENSEMBLE* IS PREPROGRAMMED TO DEAL WITH THREATS AGAINST A TRAVELER'S LIFE.

IF IVAN DIES, NO ONE WILL BE ABLE TO STOP MY SON FROM KILLING YOU.

DIES? NO, DON'T BE SILLY.

WHEN I WAS TWELVE, MY MOTHER CAUGHT ME TOUCHING A SIX-YEAR-OLD NEIGHBOR GIRL, AND IT MORTIFIES ME TO THINK BACK TO THAT DAY.

HUH?

SORRY, DID I LOSE MY TRAIN OF THOUGHT? ALERT ME IF I DO THAT AGAIN, BHOTA.

EVERY OTHER SENTENCE FEELS LIKE I'M DRIFTING OFF TO SLEEP, YOU KNOW? IT'S... *CONFUSING* BEING HERE.

I MEANT TO SAY THAT MR. TERESHKOV IS IN NO DANGER AT ALL. THE FORCE I USED AGAINST HIM WAS JUST EXCESS *STRAND ENERGY* STORED UP FROM MY BURROWING.

IT STUNNED HIM, BUT HE'LL WAKE UP WITH A VERY CLEAR HEAD... THEORETICALLY, I SUPPOSE.

I KNOW WHAT YOU ARE.

YES, YES, "I'M INSANE," RIGHT?

IF THAT'S WHAT YOU NEED TO BELIEVE, BY ALL MEANS, PLEASE BE MY GUEST.

NO, YOU'RE FROM THE *FUTURE*.

NOW THEN.

I GOT A THING AGAINST PUNCHING LADIES, BUT NOT AGAINST *SHOOTING* THEM, UNDERSTOOD?

IT WAS *HIS* IDEA! I'M A GOOD GIRL, SIR!

HE MADE ME USE DRUGS AND...AND HAVE SEX!

THANKS FOR COOPERATING, SEEING HOW I LEFT MY PIECE WITH A *FRIEND.* NAME'S BRADBURY. YOU'RE UNDER CITIZEN'S ARREST, BY THE WAY.

THAT'S BULLSHIT! YOU'RE NOT EVEN A REAL *COP?*

NOT ANYMORE.

THEN WHO THE HELL *DO* YOU WORK FOR?

THE POOR BASTARD WHO'S GONNA HAVE TO CLEAN THIS MESS UP.

HELP YOUR BOYFRIEND, MOM.

BUT WHAT ARE YOU GOING TO DO WITH--

DO AS I SAY.

IT'S ALL RIGHT, IVAN. I'M HERE.

IF I DIE... TELL BOY... I AM SORRY... ABOUT *JANUARY*...

YOU'RE GOING TO BE *FINE*. WHATEVER HAPPENED BETWEEN YOU TWO LAST JANUARY...

...YOU CAN APOLOGIZE TO MITCH YOURSELF.

DEPUTY MAYOR WYLIE! SORRY, I...I WAS JUST STRAIGHTENING OUT DOWN HERE WHILE HIZZONER WAS AWAY.

I THOUGHT YOU WERE STUCK IN AN ELEVATOR.

I GOT *UNSTUCK*, AND I NEED YOU TO GRAB NOLITA CEMAC FROM O.E.M. AND READY THE BLUE ROOM FOR AN EMERGENCY PRESS CONFERENCE.

WHAT THE HELL ARE YOU DOING?

NOW.

YES, SIR.

I'M IMPRESSED, MR. MAYOR. HAVEN'T SEEN YOU SINCE THE CONNIE GEORGES FIASCO. I DIDN'T THINK YOU'D REMEMBER MY *NAME*, MUCH LESS MY ORIENTATION.

HARD TO DO FUNDRAISING WITHOUT A GOOD MEMORY FOR THAT CRAP. I KNOW IT'S MERCENARY, BUT PEOPLE ARE MORE GENEROUS WHEN THEY FEEL LIKE YOU KNOW THEM.

YEAH, WELL, MY CHICK *DUMPED* ME LAST WEEK, SO DON'T HOLD YOUR BREATH FOR A DONATION.

I'M JUST BACK FROM INTERVIEWING YOUR MOM AND MR. TERESHKOV.

YOU'LL BE HAPPY TO KNOW THAT THEY'RE BOTH IN GOOD CONDITION, THOUGH THEY'RE EVEN MORE FUCKING CONFUSED THAN I AM.

DID YOU RUN THE PRINTS OFF THE BARREL OF THE GUN I GAVE YOU?

YEP, AND THEY'RE A MATCH FOR A GUY NAMED *AUGUSTYN ZELLER.* HE WORKS FOR A SPECIAL EFFECTS COMPANY CALLED WETA.

I *KNEW* THIS WAS ALL SOME KIND OF TRICK. HAVE YOU PICKED HIM UP YET?

YOU DON'T UNDERSTAND, SIR.

WETA IS IN *NEW ZEALAND,* WHICH IS EXACTLY WHERE MR. ZELLER HAS WORKED EVERY DAY FOR THE LAST TWO YEARS...AND YEAH, THAT INCLUDES *TODAY.*

TUESDAY, SEPTEMBER 11, 2001

Inside the Machine

HARRIS

Introduction by Brian K. Vaughan

Comic books made by more than one creator are often derogatively referred to as "assembly-line books," implying that each stage of the work is dispassionately passed from one craftsman to the next in order to churn out product as quickly as possible. And while EX MACHINA does hit stands with shocking regularity, the above description doesn't capture our process in the least.

All of the artists behind this series are close friends, and it's sometimes hard to tell where one person's job starts and another's ends. My scripts often begin with a brilliant visual idea suggested by penciller and co-creator Tony Harris during one of our regular phone calls. While Old Man Harris and I are gabbing, our inker (first the amazing Tom Feister, now the equally talented Jim Clark) might catch a small continuity error in one of the previous issue's unfinished pages, which I'll try to address in the dialogue with the help of letterer extraordinaire Jared K. Fletcher. Meanwhile, J.D. Mettler will be e-mailing all of us his incomparable colors, getting input about setting the mood for a particular scene with a specific palette.

This complex cross-country network is constantly being guided from the WildStorm offices by the tireless Ben Abernathy and Kristy Quinn.

And those are just the names you see in the credit box. Each month, our team is ably assisted by countless more people, whether it's the dedicated cast of actors Tony shoots for photo reference or the government sources who are kind enough to supply me with the inside scoop on life in City Hall. Our production is bigger and more complicated than many independent films, but everyone involved feels a responsibility beyond our individual contributions to the series, and I think it makes for a unique kind of book that feels like the work of one unified vision.

EX MACHINA has always suggested that the behind-the-scenes story is infinitely more interesting than the one the public gets to see, so it's only fitting that we finally reveal the secret inner workings of our "machine."

I hope you agree it's a great one.

- Brian K. Vaughan
Los Angeles, 2007

Inside Process:
Interior page showcase

Tony Harris is always experimenting with different techniques to push himself as an artist and excel at his craft. On his covers, he typically adds a "graywash" layer to the board following the inking stage, to add a little more depth to the finished piece. For a few issues of EX MACHINA, he experimented with this technique on the interiors as well.

What follows are the opening six pages to EX MACHINA #23, featuring script, pencils, gray-washed inks and color stages.

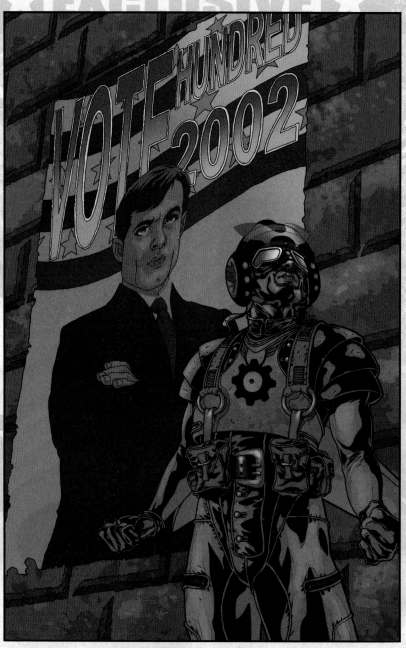

This art was commissioned by *Wizard Magazine* for a piece they were doing on the Great Machine. When printed, they cropped out the background and just ran the free-floating figure.

The Full Script for
EX MACHINA #23
Prepared for Tony Harris
and WildStorm
June 27, 2006

Page One

Page One, Panel One
 We open with this close-up of an African-American
DOORMAN, wearing a uniform like this one:

1) Doorman: You can't come in here!

Page One, Panel Two
 One of these things, same as always:

2) Date (in the style of a right-justified newspaper heading):

Monday, April 2, 2001

Page One, Panel Three
 Pull out to the largest panel of the page, as CLEVELAND
(the pot dealer from last issue) RUNS into the lobby of this quiet
old apartment building and KNOCKS his way past the startled
doorman.

3) Doorman: This is a private buil--
4) Doorman: OOF!

5) Cleveland: Help! He's trying to kill me!

Page Two

Page Two, Panel One
Cut to the revolving door entrance to this old apartment building, as the helmeted GREAT MACHINE runs inside. He left his busted jetpack in the cab, so he's wingless here.

1) Great Machine (small font, whispering): Where did he go?

Page Two, Panel Two
Pull out to the largest panel of the page for a shot of the Great Machine and the doorman, as the floored doorman points at a nearby STAIRWELL DOOR.

2) Doorman: Say again?

3) Great Machine: Where the hell did he go?

4) Doorman: Stuh… stairwell.

Page Two, Panel Three
Change angles on the two men, as the Great Machine runs for an old elevator with an "OUT OF ORDER" sign on it.

5) Great Machine (small font, whispering): -koff- -koff- Thanks.

6) Doorman: Don't bother, man!
7) Doorman: That elevator hasn't worked in years!

Page Two, Panel Four
Push in on the Great Machine, as he gives a little half-smile.

8) Great Machine (GREEN FONT/BALLOON): I think I can coax her out of retirement.

Page Three

Page Three, Panel One
Cut to the Great Machine's warehouse hideout (from Sprouse's special) where KREMLIN is talking into a microphone, while BRADBURY listens in behind him.

1) Kremlin: Mitchell, let him go!
2) Kremlin: No pusher boy is worth dying for!

Page Three, Panel Two
Cut onto the roof of the apartment building, where the Great Machine bursts out of a roof-access door.

3) Great Machine: You stick with a job until it's finished, Kremlin.

4) Electronic (tailless): But Bradbury says there is deli getting robbed two blocks from you! Those people need you more than--

Page Three, Panel Three
Pull out to the largest panel of the page. We're in the foreground with Cleveland, who is RUNNING at us, right for the EDGE of the five-story building's roof!

5) Great Machine: Cleveland, don't!

Page Three, Panel Four
Push in on the Great Machine, who yells:

6) Great Machine: You'll never make it!

Page Four

Page Four, Panel One
Cut to Cleveland, who LEAPS over a wide alleyway towards another roof across the way.

1) Cleveland: Eat dick!

Page Four, Panel Two
We're behind the Great Machine, looking over his shoulder, as he watches Cleveland LAND safely on the other roof.

2) Great Machine: Son of a…

Page Four, Panel Three
Change angles on the Great Machine, as he RUNS as fast as he can, preparing to jump just like Cleveland did.

3) Great Machine (small font, whispering): My legs are machines, my legs are machines, my legs are…

Page Four, Panel Four
Change angles for this largest panel of the page, a cool-ass shot of the wingless Mitchell JUMPING across the wide alleyway. Maybe we're down in the alley, looking up at him as he makes the leap? Whatever looks coolest, man.

No Copy

Page Five

Page Five, Panel One
Push in, as the Machine just MISSES the roof, and narrowly CATCHES the edge of it with his arms.

1) Great Machine: UNF!

Page Five, Panel Two
Pull out to a shot of both men, as Cleveland looks down at the Machine (holding on for dear life), and aims the RAYGUN he stole at his face.

2) Cleveland: Dude.
3) Cleveland: Stop. Fucking. *FOLLOWING ME!*

Page Five, Panel Three
Push in tight on the Great Machine, as his scars begin to GLOW beneath his goggles.

4) Great Machine (GREEN FONT/BALLOON): Voltage spike.

Page Five, Panel Four
Pull out to the largest panel of the page, as the raygun in Cleveland's hand suddenly EXPLODES in a burst of sparks, electrocuting him..

5) SFX: KZZZAXXXX

Page Six

Page Six, Panel One
We're with Cleveland's fallen body in the foreground of this shot. In the background, the Great Machine PULLS himself up onto the roof.

1) Cleveland: Nnn…!

Page Six, Panel Two
Pull out to the largest panel of the page for a shot of both men. The Great machine is standing over the groggy Cleveland, as Mitchell pulls out a pair of HANDCUFFS from one of his pouches.

2) Great Machine (small font, whispering): Cleveland Severtson, I'm placing you under citizen's arrest.

3) Cleveland: All this for a little grass?

4) Great Machine (small font, whispering): An apartment-full is hardly a little. Besides, you sell to children.

Page Six, Panel Three
Push in on the two men, as the Great Machine handcuffs Cleveland.

5) Cleveland: No, I sell to rich folk! I can't control who they give their shit to.
6) Cleveland: Look, I'm not a rapist! I've never murdered anybody! You can't send me to prison!

7) Great Machine (small font, whispering): I'm not. I'm sending you to the cops.

Page Six, Panel Four
This is just a shot of the exhausted Great Machine, as he matter-of-factly says:

8) Great Machine: I can't control who they give their shit to.
9) Great Machine: -koff- -koff-

Inside the Covers

Tony Harris is an Eisner-winning cover artist from his STARMAN days—and in 2006, he was again nominated for "Best Cover Artist." What follows is an Inside look into Tony's cover creation process, as he pencils, inks and colors every cover on his own, with notes from the old man himself.

#1

This was actually the second cover produced for the first issue. (More on that in a moment!) But the team felt the first version I did (which was eventually used as the cover to #4) wasn't powerful enough to be issue one's cover. I have to say, in hindsight, I agree.

This is the final cover for issue #4. As mentioned, this was originally the first issue cover.

My initial thoughts were to include a single bold word that would encompass the story inside. Later, we decided not to do this because it would fight with the logo and cover copy. I did, however, get to do this with the Lincoln cover to issue #2— effectively, as can be seen on page 105!

The ghosted city here was done totally digital and does not appear on the original. Note the super-ghosted Brooklyn Bridge at the bottom.

Here is my model for Mitchell Hundred, Jimmy Hill. He can have such an intense look when he's lit right. For this design I wanted to riff on Mitchell's multi-tasking as the Great Machine and the Mayor. So this cover represents the balance of Force (bottom pair of hands), Deliberation (middle pair), and the Scales of Justice (top pair).

I used a shot of myself here because Jimmy wasn't available. I later shot his head and inserted it, then added the skyline as an afterthought. I really wanted to play with how matted down and sweaty his hair would be under that mask and helmet on a summer day. I thought it all worked out quite well.

This might be my favorite EX MACHINA image to date. I got lucky with the design flowing properly.

I was worried when it was cut in two (to be the covers to the EX MACHINA SPECIALS) that they wouldn't work as well individually. But after some deliberation I removed the Brooklyn Bridge (pictured in the photo comp) and replaced it with the Statue of Liberty and the NYC skyline featuring the Twin Towers. Then it all came together with the addition of the field of stars. I was really pleased to hear that DC will be releasing a poster of this image!

S
P
E
C
I
A
L
S

TAG

I used different Tarot Card titles to label the different characters and the issues dealt with in the story arc featured here.

The research and decision-making on this particular cover made it especially rewarding. Plus I got to play with my son's plastic rayguns I used as reference. The juxtaposition of hero and villain on the right side of the image was the cement that brought the whole design home for me.

FACT V. FICTION

SMOKE SMOKE

Ex Machina: Concepts & Photos

These were some 3-D images of the jet pack Brian Frey built. Originally, I wanted these commissioned so that I could do full turnarounds for photo ref while drawing the Machine in action. It proved to be too time consuming, so it was easier to just keep hard copies laying around and draw the jet pack freehand whenever needed. I did, however, create the entire cover to issue #10 digitally, using one of these images with a "skin" painted on.

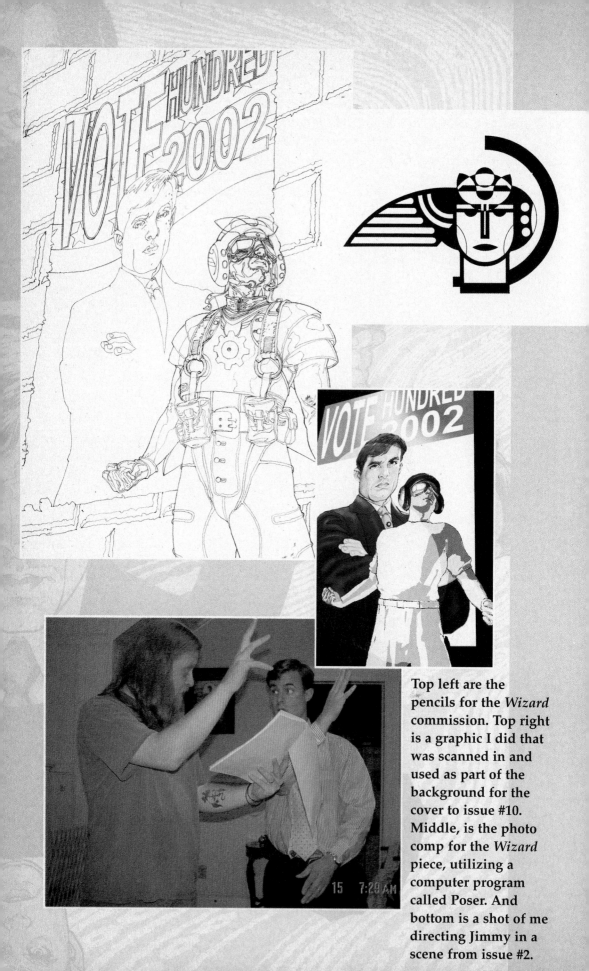

Top left are the pencils for the *Wizard* commission. Top right is a graphic I did that was scanned in and used as part of the background for the cover to issue #10. Middle, is the photo comp for the *Wizard* piece, utilizing a computer program called Poser. And bottom is a shot of me directing Jimmy in a scene from issue #2.

Jimmy Hill and Greta O'Dell
(Commissioner Angotti)
rehearsing the rooftop
beating the Great Machine
takes from Angotti in
issue 2. At the bottom is
Kremlin's aviator cap.

Afterword by
Tony Harris

There's an old saying that goes, "I'm my own worst critic." That would totally be true in my case—except for the fact that I have a wife and two children. My wife and kids, specifically my son, are my worst critics. I wouldn't have it any other way. There is an honesty to their comments that makes them pure; the kind of honesty that you can only get from those closest to you.

Back when I was drawing STARMAN for DC Comics, my editor was the legendary Archie Goodwin. Aside from the honor of working for Archie, I also felt he was the single best editor I've ever worked for. He had the same honesty about my art that my wife has. Each month when it was time for me to do the painted cover on the book, I would submit anywhere from one to three sketches for approval. Generally I would try to let Archie know—in a roundabout way—which of the sketches I was leaning toward, without tempering his input. Now here's where it gets interesting. My wife sees everything I do before it goes out the door, in every stage from sketch to pencil, ink or paint. In the four years I worked for Archie, my wife always picked the sketch that Archie would ultimately choose. Every time.

Every single time.

As an artist, it is so important to trust in your ability, your skill. But equally important are the people you surround yourself with. Your confidants. Over the years I have shared studio space with other artists, writers, painters, and friends. They came and went, and sometimes I moved on. These days, my trusted friends, co-workers, and confidants are the guys I work with on EX MACHINA. I can honestly say this is the best collaboration I've experienced in 19 years of working in comics. And as much as I never thought it would happen again, I found in Ben Abernathy the same feeling of trust and comfort that I remember fondly from the years I spent working under Archie Goodwin.

Then there is Brian K. Vaughan. What can I say that everyone else already hasn't?

It's all been said so I won't repeat it. But I can speak to what it's like to work with him. I've been blessed to work with a lot of talented writers, but this working relationship is the truest collaboration I've experienced. I came to EX MACHINA on the back end of Brian's deal with WildStorm, so it was a shock and surprise that he was so open to what I had to say and what I had to show him. The Great Machine went from being a typical superhero with a cape to the leather clad, jetpack-wearing, helmeted gimp we all love today. And once I was on board, I had some other ideas, too. I went to Brian with them and much to my surprise he liked them. I gotta say I wasn't used to that from writers; a lot of them are very guarded when it comes to their scripts and they want drawn exactly what was written. Brian wants that too, but he also wants his script interpreted. He wants to collaborate. Lucky me.

Guess who else I trust? You. I really don't have a choice. Team Machina put a book about politics in your hands, and you all "got" it. You made it fly. And all of us on the team immediately got it, too. I think that's why we all signed on so quickly. A lot of people didn't think it would work, so I wonder: how's that working out for them now, do you think?

I had hoped to give you all a special treat with this book. An inside look at the Machine. How it works, and how we work. Hopefully we did that, and right now you are twice as excited about EX MACHINA as you were before you read this. The funny part is, we just arrived at the halfway point! I realized this the other day when I started working on issue 28. We have so much more to come—so many more great stories and hopefully some creative leaps in the art. My point is, we are just getting warmed up and the future looks bright. Thanks so much for making it possible to see my dreams come true on such a great project.

- Tony Harris, 2006